Ramabai at work on her translation of the Bible into popular Marathi

Pandita Ramabai Sarasvati

Pioneer in the Movement for the Education of the Child-widow of India

By
CLEMENTINA BUTLER
*Chairman Executive Committee American
Ramabai Association*

NEW YORK   CHICAGO
Fleming H. Revell Company
LONDON AND EDINBURGH

New York: 158 Fifth Avenue
Chicago: 17 North Wabash Ave.
London: 21 Paternoster Square
Edinburgh: 75 Princes Street

Introduction

A WIDOW without resources, a Hindu widow
burdened with the handicap of religious
fanaticism and superstition which weighed
down any aspirations for betterment, and hedged
about in all avenues of effort, and yet a valiant
spirit which, recognizing a vision and a command,
went forth for its fulfillment. This was Pandita
Ramabai, the courageous soul who first saw the
crying need of the child-widow, who realized the
economic loss to the nation of setting apart a
great class by ostracism to enforced inaction; the
one who realized the right of the child to live, to
work, and to have development of her powers in
spite of the supposed curse of the gods upon her
life.

It was in 1886 that this little woman, coming
unknown and unsupported save by her own
strength of conviction, landed on these shores and
made her appeal for the child-widow of India.
Modern, bustling America hardly knew that such
a class existed, and the missionary folk who did
know were not fully aware of the weight upon the
girl-child heart of feeling condemnation because
of the belief that the curse of the gods was the

cause of the death of the boy or man to whom
she was betrothed. So great was Ramabai's conviction and so high her courage that immediate
hearing was accorded her. As she stood before
great audiences, unconscious of fear because of her
anxiety to place her message before those who
could enable her to break the bonds and let the oppressed go free, her plea found a generous re-
sponse. Friends were raised up who made the
pledge that they would back her initial experiment
for ten years till it could be proven whether it was
within the bounds of possibility to have the child-
widow of the high-castes educated and given an
opportunity for a life of usefulness.

Among those who pledged to this unique enterprise the strong support which made possible the
institution of the Shârâdâ Sadan—" Home of
Wisdom "—, we find the names of men and women
of different denominations: Edward Everett Hale,
Phillips Brooks, Lyman Abbott, Judith W. Andrews, Joseph Cook and Frances Willard.

In 1887 an Association was formed in the City
of Boston with the names of these Christian leaders
as incorporators for the purpose of establishing
this Institution. The Association has continued
not for ten years but for thirty-five, and still exists
to carry on the work. Pandita Ramabai on the
fifth of April 1922 finished her task. A reminder
of the influences which made this highly gifted and

unique personality able to cope with the immense difficulties of such a proposition, and which developed the executive ability to carry it out practically unaided, may be welcome as we review her accomplishment. For those who admire high courage and _faith_ and achievement these following pages are written.

CLEMENTINA BUTLER,
Chairman, Executive Committee,
American Ramabai Association.

Wesleyan Building, Boston.

Contents

Illustrations

I

RAMABAI'S VISION

IN the great aggregation of races and nations which we call Hindustan we find not only a multiplicity of faiths and religious customs, among which are some whose rites and customs grieve and offend us, but also some followers of these whose high ideals lift them above what is undesirable, and whose simple piety commands our sympathy, even though we may not agree with their beliefs. Such a man was Ananta Shastri Dongre, a Brahmin Pundit, liberal beyond the teachings of his sacred writings, with a vision which lifted womanhood out of the depression and inaction to which Hinduism had condemned her. His marriage, according to custom, to Lakshmibai, a child of nine years, impressed him as contrary to the best interest of his race, and her absolute illiteracy so distressed him that he determined to educate the child, a course so opposed to the cherished traditions of the Brahmins that it brought upon him ostracism and even persecution.

Finding the mind of the little wife developing under his teaching he persisted, even though it meant that he must go to live in some secluded place where his actions would not offend. Therefore he took up his abode in the forest of Gungamal, in Western India, in a spot so lonesome and remote that often the howls of wild beasts terrified the family in the dark hours of the night. In this forest home on April 23, 1858, a little daughter was born, to whom the father gave the name of Ramabai—it may be translated " Delight-giver "—and he determined that this little girl should have a chance for an education untrammelled by Hindu customs and restrictions. The child received the most tender training from both mother and father, and her memories of this life in the forest with no companions save her family and the books which they regarded as their chief treasures, remained vividly with Ramabai through her life. Ananta Shastri's fame brought many students to sit at his feet in study of the classics.

Later, poverty, resulting from the hospitality imposed upon Hindu teachers, had involved him in debt, and finally the family set out upon a pilgrimage, having no certain dwelling-place, but wandering from one sacred locality to another, receiving only the small amounts given in gratitude by students who came for instruction to the well-known Pundit. The great famine of the Madras Presidency occurred during these years of wandering and bore with terrible suffering upon the pilgrims, who, in order to please the gods, would give away what little they possessed in alms to the Brahmans, and then pray to the gods to send them gold. Ramabai's own account says: "We went to several sacred places to worship different gods and to bathe in sacred rivers and tanks, to free ourselves from sin and the curse which brought poverty on us. We prostrated ourselves before the stone and metal images of the gods, and prayed to them day and night, the burden of our prayer being that the gods would be pleased to give us wealth, learning and renown. But nothing came of this futile effort, the stone images remained as hard as ever and never answered our prayers. We knew the Vedanta, and knew also that we worshipped, not images, but some gods whom they represented. Still, all our learning and superior knowledge was of no avail. We went to the astrologers with money and other presents to know from them the minds of the gods concerning us. In this way we spent our precious time, strength, and wealth in vain. When no money was left in hand, we began to sell the valuable things belonging to us. Jewelries, costly garments, silver ware, and even the cooking vessels of brass and copper, were sold at the last and the money spent in giving alms to Brahmans, till nothing but a few silver and copper coins were left in our possession. We bought coarse rice with them, and ate very sparingly; but it did not last long. At last the day came when we had finished eating the last grain of rice, and nothing but death by starvation remained for our portion. Oh, the sorrow, the helplessness, and the disgrace of the situation!

" We assembled together to consider what we should do next, and after a long discussion came to the conclusion that it was better to go into the forest and die there than bear the disgrace of poverty among our own people; and that very night we left the house in which we were staying and entered into the great forest, determined to die. Eleven days and nights (in which we subsisted on water and leaves and a handful of wild dates) were spent in great bodily and mental pain. At last our dear old father could hold out no longer: the tortures of hunger were too much for his poor, old, weak body. He determined to drown himself in a sacred tank near by, thus to end all his earthly sufferings. It was suggested that the rest of us should either drown ourselves or break the family and go our several ways, but drowning ourselves seemed practicable. (To drown one's self in some sacred river or tank is not considered suicide by Hindus, so we felt free to put an end to our lives in that way.) Father wanted to drown himself first, so he took leave of all the members of the family one by one. I was his youngest child, and my turn came last. I shall never forget his last injunctions to me. His blind eyes could not see my face; but he held me tight in his arms, and stroking my head and cheeks, he told me in a few words, broken with emotion, to remember how he loved me, and how he taught me to do right, and never depart from the way of righteousness. His last loving command to me was to lead an honorable life, if I lived at all, and serve God. He did not know the only true God, but served the—to him—unknown God with all his heart and strength; and he was very desirous that his children should serve Him to the last. 'Remember, my child,' he said, 'you are my youngest, my most beloved child: I have given you into the hands of our God. You are His, and to Him alone you must belong, and serve Him all your life.'

"While we were placed in such a bewildering situation the merciful God, who so often prevents His sinful children from rushing headlong into the deep pit of sin, came to our rescue. He kept us from the dreadful act of being witnesses to the suicide of our own beloved father. God put a noble thought into the heart of my brother, who said he could not bear to see the sad sight. He would give up all caste pride and go to work to support our old parents; and, as father was unable to walk, he said he would carry him down the mountain into the nearest village, and then go to work. He made his intentions known to father, and begged him not to drown himself in the sacred tank. So the question was settled for that time. Our hearts were gladdened, and we prepared to start from the forest; and yet we wished very

much that a tiger, a great snake, or some other
wild animal would put an end to our lives. We
were too weak to move, and too proud to beg or
work to earn a livelihood. But the resolution was
made, and we dragged ourselves out of the jungle
as best we could.

" It took us nearly two days to come out of the
forest into a village at the foot of the mountain.
Father suffered intensely throughout this time.
Weakness, caused by starvation and the hardships
of the life in the wilderness, hastened his death.
We took shelter in a temple, but the Brahman
priests would not let us stay there. They had no
pity for the weak and helpless. So we were
obliged again to move from the temple and go out
of the village into the ruins of an old temple,
where no one but the wild animals dwelt in the
night. There we stayed for four days. A young
Brahman, seeing the helplessness of our situation,
gave us some food. The same day my father was
attacked by fever from which he did not recover."

After the death of her father and mother
Ramabai, with her brother, travelled throughout
India until they arrived in Calcutta, where opportunity came for her to take advantage of her
scholarship. The story of her knowledge and her
views on the emancipation and education of woman
were received with enthusiasm by some Hindus,
who delighted to hear the holy Sanscrit from a
woman's lips. Her fame had reached Calcutta,

and a formal invitation was given for her to lecture in that great city before the assembled Pundits. Her remarkable scholarship and especially her thorough knowledge of the Sanscrit Holy Books so delighted these scholars that they called a public assembly in the Town Hall of Calcutta and conferred upon her the highest title possible in India for a woman—" Sarasvati," " Goddess of Wisdom." She was twenty-two at this time and unmarried, for her father had refused the offers which came to him from the time she was nine, stating that she was to be a student; this refusal to conform to the caste customs being partly responsible for his misfortunes. Her brother's devotion and aid was sufficient up to this time, and they continued together the work their father had so well begun.

Again sorrow struck her heart in the death of her brother, whose constitution had been underminded by the ravages of famine. She was left alone in the world, but a few months later married a Bengali gentleman, Bepin Bihari Medhavi, a graduate of Calcutta University. As each was too advanced for the popular Hinduism of the day, they were united by the civil marriage rite. After nineteen months of happy married life her husband died, leaving her with a little daughter, whom they had named Manorama (Heart's Joy). She continued her lectures, and formed soon after a society of ladies known as the Arya Mahila Somaj, whose object was the promotion of education among native women and the discouragement of child-marriage. She then went from city to city throughout the Bombay Presidency, establishing branch societies and arousing the people by her eloquent appeals.

Ramabai now realized that she herself needed training to enable her to prosecute with success her work among the women of India on behalf of education. Then too, as she had in her experience become conscious of God's guidance, her spirit was possessed of that unrest which is the solemn movement of the soul Godward, seeking the Lord, if haply she (they) might feel after Him and find Him. "I felt a restless desire to go to England," she writes. "I could not have done this unless I had felt that my faith in God had become strong: it is such a great step for a Hindu woman to cross the sea; one cuts one's self always off from one's people. But the voice came to me, as to Abraham. I went forth, not knowing whither I went." Before leaving India Ramabai wrote a book on Morals for Women, which furnished the money for her passage. Friends were raised up for her in England, where she saw for the first time Christianity at work. One thing that impressed her was the rescue work for women as a new thing in religion, something which not only rewarded the good and virtuous, but attempted even to lift the fallen; and as a result of her observations she and her little daughter were baptized in the Church of England in 1883. Having acquired English in a year of study in the Home of St. Mary at Wantage, she secured a position as Professor of Sanskrit at the Women's College at Cheltenham, where she also entered as a student of mathematics, science, and English literature.

In 1886 she was attracted to America, in order to witness the graduation of her cousin, Mrs. Joshee, from the Women's Medical College in Philadelphia. Soon after her arrival here she wrote:—

" I am deeply impressed by and interested in the work of Western women, who seem to have one common aim; namely, the good of their fellow-beings. It is my dream some day to tell my countrywomen, in their own languages, this wonderful story, in the hope that the recital may awaken in their hearts a desire to do likewise."

As her contact with a public educational system, which included girls as well as boys, was prolonged, her old desire to benefit her countrywomen by forming schools which combined the training of the hand with that of the head revived, and, forsaking plans which regarded only the higher education of the few women in government high schools or colleges in India, she concentrated her thoughts upon native schools founded by and for native women. Her first public address was on March 2, 1886, in the parlor of the Y. M. C. A., in Philadelphia, where for three-quarters of an hour she

held the attention of the audience as she spoke of
the condition and needs of her sex, the life and re-
lations of Hindu womanhood, and made an appeal
for sympathy in her proposed work. Not long
after this she came to Boston and appeared on the
platform of Tremont Temple. Many friends were
raised up for her, and finally, Dec. 13, 1887, the
Ramabai Association was formed, with the object
of giving education to high-caste child widows of
India. Her friends at different places organized
Circles which pledged themselves to give annually
for the space of ten years a sum of money with
which she might establish a home to train Hindu
widows, especially the child widows from high-
caste homes, and so enable them to gain an independent livelihood. She pledged herself to adhere
in her mode of living to native customs. In regard
to the project, she said: "I am fully aware of the
great responsibility, the trial, and it may be the
failure, it will involve; but, as some one must make
a beginning, I am resolved to try, trusting that God,
who knows the need of my countrywomen, will
raise up able workers to forward this cause,
whether I succeed in it or not. The great majority
of my country people being bitterly opposed to the
education of women, there is little hope of my getting from them either good words or pecuniary
aid."

Audiences in Boston are accustomed to strange
peoples and unusual plans, but no one who was

Ramabai on her first visit to America in 1886.

present that day can ever forget the slight figure of the little widow in her white garb and with the close shaven head indicative of her despised estate, as she gave her burning plea for justice for the child-widow of India, that little one who, betrothed in infancy, and before the final ceremony was performed was condemned to the ignominy of life long widowhood because of the death of the boy or man she had never seen, betrothal being considered binding the girl in the case. Such a condition appeared in no country on earth save in Hindustan and, outside of Christian help, there was no remedy.

The touching appeal found its way to the hearts of many who pledged themselves for ten years support of Ramabai's enterprise; and so, with her dream fulfilled, the Pundita started back, no longer oppressed with the knowledge of tragic conditions without any prospect for alleviation in sight. Her reception in India was more cordial than she dared to hope. It was understood that the new School was to be non-sectarian, which the Hindus took to mean non-Christian. This view made difficulties of which we will speak later.

In March, 1889, the Shârâdâ Sadan (the Home of Wisdom) was opened in Bombay. Ramabai had returned from her native land after nearly seven years' absence, no longer a poor, friendless, homeless widow, but a leader supported by hundreds—no, by thousands—of sympathetic hearts in

America and England as she began her great work
for the high-caste girls and widows in that section
of India. At the dedication of the school a high-
caste Hindu lady had been induced to take the
chair. A newspaper of Bombay states that this
was the first time that an Indian lady had ever pre-
sided on such an important occasion. Pandita
Ramabai gave an account of her travels and her
plans for the benefit of her fellow countrywomen,
and stated the principles on which she should con-
duct her school, following with an earnest appeal
to her countrymen for their sympathy and support.
The Sadan was opened that very afternoon, with
one student, a child widow, who had suffered much
since her betrothed husband had died, so that she
had been considering suicide. Another came soon,
and by the end of the first quarter twenty-two students were under Ramabai's influence. " Already,"
Pandita Ramabai writes, " I can see a change in
the impish natures of my girls. They seem to feel
their responsibility. We have happy times in the
evenings when all the girls come into my room and
we sing together as best we can. We have no love
songs to sing, no comic bits to say; but we sing
hymns and feel quite contented. You see, they do
not allow women to sing: they think it is a bad
thing in a housewife. But we are getting unruly
in this school of ours. We are going to turn the
tide, and make it a good and honorable taste."

An Advisory Board was formed in India, carrying such names as Professor Ramakrishna Bhandarkar, Mr. Justice Telang, and others. In the early days Ramabai had full opportunity to report to us the life stories of her pupils. The pathetic stories that follow speak for themselves:—

"A child widow of thirteen was brought to the school by her father. She was betrothed when just emerging from babyhood, and taken to live with her mother-in-law. She never knew a child's happiness, and, when her husband died, the treatment she received became cruel in the extreme. Constantly taunted with having killed her husband by some sin committed in a former existence, starved, beaten, her body often balanced through a ring suspended from the ceiling, she became prematurely old. When her father could bear the sight no longer, and took her to Ramabai, the light had gone out of her large dark eyes, her head and shoulders were bowed as under a great burden. Ramabai's heart ached for the poor child, and she took her in. They played with her, sang to her little songs, tried to make her forget her misery, and succeeded. Soon strength returned to her limbs, the light to her eyes, and her whole expression changed as she felt the joy of being a free and happy child. She proves to be an intelligent and diligent pupil."

"The story of Gangabai is equally sad. She was a widow at fifteen, an ignorant child who could neither read nor write. She was defrauded by her brother-in-law of all her jewels and the movable property of her husband, to which she was entitled by the laws of that Presidency. Her fine linen was replaced by the coarse garment which was to be henceforth the badge of shame. Her head was shaven, and every possible indignity was heaped upon her. She was forced to beg for work and food, or starve. Work she could not get. Filth instead of food was thrown into her little basket. Mocking, taunting words were the only answers to her piteous appeals. Three times she resolved to put an end to her miserable existence, but the fear of another incarnation into womanhood restrained her. She heard of Ramabai's school and came to it, notwithstanding the curses of her people, who threatened her with excommunication, loss of caste and religion, and with all the plagues they could invoke. She came and was happy, praying night and morning that, when born again, it might be among the birds, and not a woman."

In 1891 the institution was removed to Poona, where a fine building was purchased for its use, costing $15,000. It was a veritable haven of rest for the despised child-widows, a door of opportunity for an honorable and happy life. At the dedication of this new building Ramabai had the joy of having with her Mrs. Andrews, who was chairman of the Board of Managers of the Association, and was a mother beloved to this her Indian daughter in her unceasing care and efforts for the successful prosecution of her enterprise.

The child-widow described with the brass water pots.

Tara, a child-widow eleven years old. She was branded with hot irons.

At the beginning of her school Ramabai's idea was to have it absolutely non-sectarian, to allow freedom for all faiths and caste observances. This was, and still is, the policy of the school; but Ramabai's own Christian life had so grown from year to year in depth and sweetness, and was such an example before the eyes of her girls, that many of them became Christians. This caused a loss of sympathy with the Hindu members of our Advisory Board, and it was feared by some members of the Association here that she was departing from the policy which was understood from the beginning, of remaining neutral, and exerting no compulsion on the Hindu women to leave their ancestral faith. (Ramabai stated, and we believe her to have kept the vow, that she would not interfere with the religious preferences of her pupils; but such a life as hers, so consecrated in its Christian service, has not failed to attract, so that the very large majority of those under her care have become earnest Christians.) In 1892 such opposition arose because of these events that one of the daily papers of the city stated, " The Shârada Sadan has received its death blow," and many of her pupils were removed from her school for fear of their becoming Christians. Anonymous letters threatened Ramabai's life; papers became abusive, and even indecent; the Advisory Board in India resigned, and circulars were sent to parents and guardians advising the withdrawal of the widows.

But Ramabai's policy was not changed. She refused to close her door when holding her family prayers with her daughter at five o'clock in the morning. From that time on she has been unhampered in her absolute freedom of worship. During a visit to Mukti in 1906 I found some in the Home still keeping their caste rules as orthodox Hindus; but the large majority, having received from this institution the freedom which Christianity allows in educational and social matters, have desired to accept this liberty in things religious.

The need for such an institution had been set before the public by Ramabai in her book, The High-Caste Hindu Widow, to which a very warm reception was given, and the London Atheneum reviewing it stated: " The new institution has, we understand, received the support of two of the most distinguished scholars of India, Ramkrishna Bhandarkar and Kasenath Telang. After all the most telling argument for the scheme is the story of Ramabai's life, spent as it has been in the face of severe trials. We are glad to note that at the recent Oriental Congress at Christiania the Pundita's name was selected by Professor Max Muller in his published address to place with those of Ram Mohum Roy, Keshub Chunder Sen and Nilakan Tagore as representatives of modern Indian progress."

The two whose names are thus so highly honored, Dr. Bhandarkar and Justice Telang were both kind enough to allow their names to be on the Advisory Board for the Shâradâ Sadan during its first three years of existence, and until a number of conversions to Christianity occurred when they withdrew their names.

II

THUS SAITH THE LAW!

IN order that we may understand something
of the contrast between Ramabai's aims for
her sisters and the attitude of Hinduism towards them, we should note the limitations placed
upon womanhood by the laws of Manu, and quoted
by the Pundita in her book—The High Caste
Hindu Woman—(now unhappily out of print but
available in missionary libraries), and in judging
between her statements and those of certain people
who attempt to gloss over the truth of this matter, let us recall the fact that she was, by the assembled pundits of Calcutta, entitled Sarasvati, due
to her knowledge of the sacred books of their faith,
therefore she speaks with authority unquestionable.
While recognizing frankly that caste originated in
the idea of the economic division of labor, she
states—P. 35 "that when caste became an article
of the Hindu faith it assumed the formidable pro-
portions which now prevail everywhere in India."
" The Vedas are believed by the devout Hindu to
be the eternal self-existing Word of God revealed
by Him to different sages, and besides the Vedas
there were more than twenty-five books of sacred

law on which are based the principal customs and religious institutions of the Hindus. Among these the Code of Manu ranks highest and is believed to be very sacred, second to nothing but the Vedas themselves."

"Although Manu and the other law givers differ greatly on many points, they all agree on things concerning women. According to this sacred law a woman's life is divided into three parts, viz.: 1, Childhood, 2, Young or married life, and 3, Widowhood or old age.

"Hear now the duties of women.

"By a girl, by a young woman or even by an aged one, nothing must be done independently even in her own house.

"In childhood a female must be subject to her father, in youth to her husband, and when her lord is dead, to her sons; a woman must never be independent.

"Though destitute of virtue, or seeking pleasure elsewhere or devoid of good qualities, yet a husband must be constantly worshipped as a god by a faithful wife." Manu V 147-156.

"A barren wife may be superseded in the eighth year, she whose children all die in the tenth, she who bears only daughters in the eleventh, but she who is quarrelsome without delay."—Manu IX 78.

Ramabai comments on the above:

"But no such provision is made for the woman; on the contrary she must remain with and revere her husband as a god even though he be destitute of virtue and seek pleasure elsewhere, or be devoid of good qualities, addicted to evil passion, fond of spirituous liquors, or diseased and what not!

"Our Aryan Hindus did and still do honor women to a certain extent. Although the woman is looked upon as an inferior being, the mother is nevertheless the chief person and worthy to receive all honor from the son. The mother is the queen of the son's household; she wields great power there and is generally obeyed as the head of the family by her sons and daughters-in-law. But there is a reverse side to the shield which should not be left unobserved. This is best studied in the Laws of Manu, as all Hindus with a few exceptions believe implicitly what that lawgiver says about women:—in Chap. IX 18.

"It is the nature of women to seduce men in this world; for that reason the wise are never unguarded in the company of females.

"For women are able to lead astray in this world not only a fool, but even a learned man.

"For women no sacramental rite is performed with the sacred texts, thus the law is settled. Women who are destitute of the knowledge of the Vedic texts are as impure as falsehood itself."

"Those who diligently and impartially read the Sanscrit literature in the original cannot fail to recognize the Lawgiver and as one of those who

have done their best to make woman a hateful being in the world's eye. To employ her in house-
keeping and kindred occupation is thought to be
the only means of keeping her out of mischief, the
blessed enjoyment of literary culture being denied
her. She is forbidden to read the sacred scrip-
tures, she has no right to pronounce a single syllable of them. To appease her uncultivated low
kind of desire by giving her ornament to adorn
her person and by giving her dainty food, together
with an occasional bow which costs nothing, are
the highest honors to which a Hindu woman is
entitled. She, the loving mother, the devoted wife,
the tender sister and affectionate daughter is
never fit for independence and is as impure as
falsehood itself."

"I can say truthfully I have never read any
sacred book in Sanscrit literature without meeting
this hateful kind of sentiment about women. True,
they contain here and there a kind word about
them, but such words seem to me a heartless mock-
ery after having charged them as a class with crime
and evil deeds.

"Profane literature is by no means less severe
or more respectful towards women. I quote from
the ethical teachings, part of a catechism and also
a few proverbs:

Q. What is cruel?
A. The heart of the viper.
Q. What is more cruel than that?

A. The heart of a woman.

Q. What is the cruelest of all?

A. The heart of a sonless, penniless widow.

A catechism on moral subjects written by a Hindu gentleman of high literary reputation says:

Q. What is the chief gate to hell?

A. A woman.

Q. What bewitches like wine?

A. A woman.

Q. Who is the wisest of the wise?

A. He who has not been deceived by women, who may be compared to maligant fiends.

Q. What are fetters to men?

A. Women.

Q. What is that which cannot be trusted?

A. Women.

Q. What poison is that which appears like nectar?

A. Women.

Some popular proverbs:

Never put your trust in women.

Women's counsel leads to destruction.

Woman is a great whirlpool of suspicion, a dwelling place of vices, full of deceits, a hindrance in the way of heaven, a gate of hell."

" Having illustrated the popular belief about woman's nature, I now proceed to state woman's religion. Virtues such as truthfulness, forbearance, purity of heart and uprightness, are common to men and women, but religion as the word is commonly understood had two distinct natures in the Hindu law, the masculine and the feminine. The sum and substance of the latter may be given in a few words: To look upon her husband as a god, to hope for salvation only through him, to be obedient to him in all things, never to covet independence, never to do anything but that which is approved by law and custom.

" A faithful wife who desires to dwell after death with her husband must never do anything which might displease him who took her hand whether he be alive or dead. Manu V, 147-156.

" By violating her duty towards her husband a wife is disgraced in this world—after death she enters the womb of a jackal and is tormented by diseases—the punishment of her sins.

" She who, controlling her thoughts, words and deeds never slights her lord, resides after death with her husband in heaven and is called a virtuous wife. Manu V, 164.

We now come to the worst and most dreaded period of a high caste woman's life. Throughout India widowhood is regarded as the punishment of a horrible crime or crimes committed in her former existence upon earth. Disobedience and disloyalty to the husband, or murdering him in an earlier existence are the chief crimes punished in the present by widowhood.

" If the widow be a mother of sons she is not usually a pitiable object, although she is certainly

looked upon as a sinner, yet social abuse and hatred
are greatly diminished by virtue of the fact that
she is the mother of superior beings. Next in
rank to her stands the ancient widow, because a
virtuous aged widow who has bravely withstood
the thousand temptations and persecutions of her
lot commands an involuntary respect from all
people, to which may be added the honor given to
old age quite independent of the individual. The
widow mother of girls is treated indifferently and
sometimes with genuine hatred, especially so if
her daughters have not been given in marriage in
her husband's lifetime. But it is the child-widow
or a childless young widow upon whom in an
especial manner falls the abuse and hatred of the
community as the greatest criminal upon whom
Heaven's judgment has been pronounced.

" In ancient times the Code of Manu was yet
in the dark future and when the priesthood had
not yet mutilated the original Vedic text, re-
marriage was in existence. It may be briefly
stated: The rite of child marriage made many a
child a widow before she knew what marriage
was, and her husband having died sonless had no
right to enter heaven and enjoy immortality, for
the father obtains immortality if he sees the face
of a living son. Endless are the worlds of those
who have no sons; there is no place for the man
who is destitute of male offspring.

" In order that these departed husbands might

attain the abode of the blessed, the ancient sages invented the custom of " Appointment," by which the Hindu Aryans raised up seed for the deceased husbands. The brother, cousin or other kinsman successively was appointed to raise up offspring to the dead. The desired issue having been obtained, any intercourse between the appointed persons was thenceforth considered illegal and sinful. The woman still remained the widow of her deceased husband and the children were considered his heirs. Later on the custom of Appointment was gradually discouraged in spite of the Vedic text already quoted—" There is no place for the man who is destitute of male offspring."

The duties of a widow are thus described by Manu:

" At her pleasure let her emaciate her body by living on pure flowers, roots and fruits; but she must never mention the name of another man after her husband dies."

" Until death let her be patient of hardships, self controlled, chaste, and strive to fulfill that most excellent duty for wives who have one husband only." Manu V, 157.

" Nor is a second husband anywhere prescribed for virtuous women." Manu V, 162.

The self-immolation of widows on the deceased husband's pyre was evidently a custom invented by the priesthood after the Code of Manu was compiled. The law taught in the schools of Apastamba,

Asvalayana and others older than Manu do not
mention it, neither does the code of Manu. The
code of Vishnu, which is comparatively recent,
says that a woman "after the death of her husband should either lead a virtuous life or ascend
the funeral pyre of her husband."

The Casi Candam says "If matrons who have
put off glittering ornaments of gold (otherwise
widows) still wear their hair in unshortened locks,
the ministers of the fiery eyed Yama shall bind
with cords the husband of her desire."

Ramabai continues:—

"It is very difficult to ascertain the motives of
those who invented the terrible custom of the so-
called Suttee, which was regarded as a sublimely
meritorious act. As Manu, the greatest authority
next to the Vedas, did not sanction this sacrifice,
the priests saw the necessity of producing some text
which would overcome the natural fears of the
widow as well as silence the critic who should re-
fuse to allow such a horrid rite without strong
authority. So the priests said there was a text in
the Rig-veda which, according to their own render-
ing, reads thus:—

"'Om! let these women, not to be widowed, good
wives, adorned with collyrium, holding clarified
butter, consign themselves to the fire! Immortal,
not childless, not husbandless, well adorned with
gems, let them pass into the fire whose original ele-
ment is water.'

"Here was an authority greater than that of Manu or any other law giver. The priests and their allies pictured heaven in the most beautiful colors and described various enjoyments so vividly that the poor widow became madly impatient to get to the blessed place in company with her departed husband. Not only was the woman assured of her getting into heaven by this sublime act, but also that by this great sacrifice she would secure salvation to herself and her husband and to their families to the seventh generation. Be they ever so sinful, they would surely attain the highest bliss in heaven. Who would not sacrifice herself if she were sure of such a result to herself and to her loved ones? Besides this, she was conscious of the miseries and degradation to which she would be subjected now that she had survived her husband. The momentary agony of suffcation in the flames was nothing compared to her lot as a widow. She gladly consented and voluntarily offered herself to please the gods and men. The rite of Suttee is thus described by Sir Edwin Arnold:—

"'The widow bathed, put on new and bright garments, and holding Kusha grass in her left hand sipped water from her right palm, scattered some Tilla grains and then, looking eastward quietly said "Om! on this day I, such and such a one, of such a family, die in the fire, that I may meet Arundhati, and reside in Svarga; that the years of my sojourn there may be as many as the hairs upon my hus-

band, many scores multiplied; that I may enjoy
with him the facilities of heaven, and bless my ma-
ternal and paternal ancestors, and those of my
lord's line; that praised by Apsarasas, I may go far
through the fourteen regions of Indra; that pardon
may be given to my lord's sins whether he have
ever killed a Brahman, broken the laws of gratitude
and truth, or slain his friend. Now I do ascend
this funeral pyre of my husband, and I call upon
you, guardians of the eight regions of the world,
of sun, moon, air, of the fire, the ether, the earth,
and the water, and my own soul. Yama, King of
death, and you, Day, Night and Twilight, witness
that I die for my beloved, by his side upon his
funeral pyre." Is it wonderful that the passage of
the Sati to her couch of flame was like a public
festival, that the sick and sorrowful prayed her to
touch them with her little, fearless, conquering
hand, that criminals were let loose if she looked
upon them, that the horse which carried her was
never used again for earthly service?

" The act was supposed to be altogether a volun-
tary one, and no doubt it was so in many cases.
Some died for the love stronger than death which
they cherished for their husbands. Some died not
because they had been happy in this world, but because they believed with all the heart that they
should be made happy hereafter. Some to obtain
great renown, for tombstones and monuments were
erected to those who thus died, and afterwards the

names were inscribed on the long list of family gods; others again, to escape the thousand temptations, and sins and miseries which they knew would fall to their lot as widows. Those who from pure ambition or from momentary impulse, declared their intentions thus to die, very often shrank from the fearful altar; no sooner did they feel the heat of the flames than they tried to leap down and escape the terrible fate; but it was too late. They had taken the solemn oath which must never be broken, priests and other men were at hand to force them to remount the pyre. In Bengal, where this custom was most in practice, countless, fearful tragedies of this description occurred even after British rule was long established there. Christian missionaries petitioned the government to abolish this inhuman custom, but they were told that the social and religious customs of the people constituted no part of the business of the government, and that their rule in India might be endangered by such interference. The custom went on unmolected until the first quarter of the present century, when a man from among the Hindus, Raja Ram Mohun Roy, set his face against it, and declared that it was not sanctioned by the Veda as the priests claimed. He wrote many books on this subject, showing the wickedness of the act, and with the noble co-operation of a few friends, he succeeded at last in getting the government to abolish it. Lord William Bentinck, when Governor-general of

India, had the moral courage to enact the famous law of 1829, prohibiting the Suttee rite within British domains, and holding as criminals, subject to capital punishment, those who countenanced it. But it was not until 1844 that the law had any effect upon orthodox Hindu minds.

"The Rig-Veda," says Max Muller, "so far from enforcing the burning of widows, shows clearly that the custom was not sanctioned during the earliest period of Indian history. According to the hymns of the Rig-veda, and the Vedic ceremonial contained in the Grihya-sutras, the wife accompanies the corpse of her husband to the funeral pyre, but she is there addressed with a verse taken from the Rig-veda, and ordered to leave her husband and to return to the world of the living."

" 'Rise, woman,' it is said, 'come to the world of life, thou sleepest nigh unto him whose life is gone. Come to us. Thou hast thus fulfilled the duties of a wife to the husband, who once took thy hand and made thee a mother." It was by falsifying the single syllable that the unscrupulous priests managed to change entirely the meaning of the whole verse.

"Throughout India, now that the Suttee rite, partly by the will of the people and partly by the law of the Empire, is prohibited, many good people feel easy in their minds, thinking the Hindu widow has been delivered from the hand of her terrible fate, but little do they realize the true state of affairs. Throughout India, except in the northwestern provinces, women are put to the severest trial imaginable after the husband's death. They are deprived of every gold and silver ornament, of the bright-colored garments, and of all the things they love to have about or on their persons. Among the Brahmins of Deccan the heads of all widows must be shaved regularly every fortnight. What woman is there who does not love the wealth of soft and glossy hair with which nature has so generously decorated her head? A Hindu woman thinks it worse than death to lose her beautiful hair. The widow must wear a single coarse garment, white, red or brown. She must eat only one meal during the 24 hours. She must never take part in the family feasts and jubilees with others. A man thinks it unlucky to behold a widow's face. He will postpone his journey if his path happens to be crossed by a widow at the time of his departure.

" A widow is called an inauspicious thing. The name ' Rand,' by which she is generally known, is the same that is borne by a Nautch girl or a harlot. The relatives of the young widow's husband are always ready to call her bad names. There is scarcely a day of her life in which she is not cursed by these people as the cause of their beloved's death. There may be exceptions to this rule, but unhappily they are not many. The young widow is always looked upon with suspicion for fear that she may bring disgrace upon the family. The purpose of

disfiguring her by shaving her head, by not allowing her ornaments or bright, beautiful garments is
to render her less attractive to a man's eye. Not
allowing her to eat more than once a day and com-
pelling her to abstain from food altogether on
sacred days is a part of the discipline by which to
mortify her youthful nature and desire. Her life,
then, destitute as it is of the least literary knowledge, void of all hope, empty of every pleasure and
social advantage, becomes intolerable, a curse to
herself and to society at large."

Ramabai gave in her book, The High Caste
Hindu Woman, the numbers of such unfortu-
nates in her country as approximately twenty-three
million widows, of whom ten thousand were under
four years of age and fifty-one thousand between
five and nine years. This is a more moderate
estimate than that given by later census figures.

" It is often asked why the number of widows
is so very large, to which question there are two
conclusive answers. First, young girls and even
infants are often given in marriage to old men,
who soon dying leave the young brides widows
forever. Second, as an unmarried girl is a disgrace to the entire family the poorest father will
pay whatever sum he can collect to almost any man
who will marry his child. Therefore, in some parts
of India, men have made it a trade to go from
town to town, marry the young girls offered to
them and collect the fees for their support. These

Kulin Brahmins may leave fifty or one hundred child-widows, who never saw his face after the marriage rites were performed. Happily for India, this practice is growing in disfavor.

"We are told that there are no infant marriages. An answer to this statement is found in the following extract from the Mysore Census Commissioner's Report, a report for one district alone. In the first year of their existence, seventy-four Hindoo female children were carried by their parents through the forms of marriage. Children of both sexes figure on the matrimonial stage in their second year, although the girls outnumbered the boys. In the third year the proportion is still higher, while in the whole period from one to five years, five hundred and twelve boy husbands against eleven thousand one hundred and seventy-five girl wives are recorded as having been put through the travesty of the sacred rite of marriage. A still greater disproportion is presented in the next quin-quennial period, which gives as many as 180,947 child wives against 8,173 boy husbands." An editor of the native paper commented on this report as follows: "One cannot but exclaim 'Horror!' at the sight of these figures. Think of seventy-four baby wives, or rather their literally infant wives. *We must be saved from ourselves in spite of ourselves.* But who is to be our savior?"

To this cry of one of the more enlightened of

India's people we must answer that the first who walked the difficult pathway of protest against this entrenched injustice and wrong was Pundita Ramabai! She continues:—

" We are told that the life of the child widow is not so hard and pitiless as represented. That the majority have happy homes and they yield cheerfully, bravely to the restrictions their custom or religion places upon them. If so, why are the shaven heads and the coarse white garments badges of shame? Why are the bodies emaciated and disfigured by cruel blows? Why the sullen, joyless expression of the face? Why so many suicides and lives of shame? Listen to the pitiful histories of some of the inmates of the Shâradâ Sadan who bear the white marks of hot iron on their heads, white scars made by sharp fingernails meeting in the tender flesh of the face, or look at the expression on the face of one of the two thousand widows kept in the temples of Brindaban, and Ramabai's zeal on their behalf is not for a moment to be considered excessive.

Hearing of some presentation of Hinduism made to Americans Ramabai wrote, " I beg my western sisters not to be satisfied at looking at the outside beauty of the grand philosophies, and not to be charmed with hearing the interesting discourses about educated men, but to open the trap doors of the great monuments of ancient Hindoo intellect and enter into the dark cellars where they will see

the real workings of these philosophies. Let them
come to India, and live among us. Let them go
to the sacred places where countless pilgrims
throng yearly. Let them go round Jagannáth
Puri, Benares, Gaya, Allahabad, Muttra, Bindra-
ban, Dwarka, Pandharpur, Udipi, Tirpatty, and
such other sacred cities, the strongholds of Hinduism and seats of sacred learning, where the Ma-
hatmas and Sadhus dwell and where the ' sublime '
philosophies are daily taught and devoutly followed. The thousands of priests, men learned in
sacred law, who are the spiritual rulers and guides
of our people, who neglect and oppress the widows
and devour widows' houses. I have gone to many
of the so-called sacred places and have seen enough
of these possessors of superior Hindoo spirituality,
who oppress the widows and trample the poor, ignorant low caste people under their feet. They
have deprived the widows of their birthright to
enjoy pure life and lawful happiness. They send
out hundreds of emissaries to look for young
widows and bring them by thousands to the sacred
cities to rob them of their money and their virtue.
They entice the poor, ignorant women to leave
their own houses to live in the Kshetras,—i e, the
Holy Places,—and then after robbing them of their
belongings, tempt them to yield to their unholy
desires. They shut the young, helpless widows
into their large Mathas (Monasteries) hire them
out to wicked men, as long as they can get money,

and when the poor, miserable slaves are no longer pleasing, they turn them out to beg their livelihood, to suffer the horrible consequence of sin, to carry the burden of shame and finally to die the death worse than that of a starved street dog! The so-called sacred places,—those veritable hells on earth, have become the graveyard of countless widows and orphans. Thousands upon thousands of young widows are suffering untold misery and dying helpless each year throughout this land, but not a philosopher or Mahatma has come out boldly to champion their cause. If anything has been done by anybody at all, it has been done by those people who have come under the direct influence of Christianity. Let my western sisters be charmed by the books and poems that they read; there are many hard and bitter facts which we have to accept and to feel!"

It may be asked why Ramabai presumes to speak so definitely about these practices. As a scholar she might have been mislead or from hearsay she might have received misinformation, but in order that she might know for herself the truth of the matter, she made a tour through India, visiting the principal shrine cities—her widow's garb giving her access to many places which a foreigner might never enter. It is refreshing too to find that she was not only willing to tell the truth about her own people, but that she knew the history of her own beloved land. If any have received the im-

pression that India was free before the coming of
the British as has recently been stated on the public platform of our leading cities, let them read
Ramabai's description of one of the exquisite palaces of the Great Moguls, whose power throttled
India from the Moslem throne for over a thousand years. In company with Mrs. Judith W.
Andrews, then Chairman of the Executive Committee of the Ramabai Association, she visited
Delhi and Agra. She wrote:—" At Agra we saw
the great Khas Mahal, or the Emperor's private
palace, where he kept hundreds of beautiful women
shut up for life. The guide showed us the Rani's
private rooms, the gardens and the grand marble
buildings once occupied by the kings and the
queens. He also showed us the beautiful pleasure
tower called the Saman Burj, Jasmine Tower.
Visitors are shown all that is beautiful there, and
they go away carrying very pleasant impressions
of Agra. I was not satisfied by seeing the outside beauty of ' those poems in marble,' but wished
to see the dungeons where the unfortunate women
used to be confined and hanged at the pleasure of
the king. The guide at first denied the existence of
such places, but finaly, on obtaining the promise to
get a little more money for his trouble he consented to show the dungeons. He opened a trap
door on one side and guided us about, showing us
the many small and large underground rooms
where the queens who had incurred the king's dis-

pleasure used to be shut up, tortured and starved, until it pleased his majesty to set them free. The guide then lighted a big torch and took us to the farthest end of the prison into a room underneath the Jasmine tower. It was a dark, octagonal room, with a deep pit in the center, and a big beam placed in the wall, right over the pit. This beam, beautifully carved, served for hanging the unfortunate women of the zanana, who had by some unknown cause fallen under the king's displeasure, and had to suffer such a cruel death. Their lifeless bodies were let down into the pit, when the stream carried them to the waters of the Jumna, where the bodies were eated by crocodiles. Thus the poor, miserable wives of the Mogul emperors suffered torture and death in that dark hell pit, under that pleasure gallery, while their cruel masters and rivals sang songs, enjoyed life, and made merry, in the beautifully decorated Jasmine Tower above. I think but little of those lovely palaces, but always remember that dark room."

Lest any should imagine that Ramabai exaggerated, we will read what Doctor Bhandarkar, Vice Chancellor of Bombay University, an enlightened Hindoo who never professed Christianity, but who was one of the strong supporters of the Shâradâ Sadan, said before the Indian National Conference in its fifth meeting, where 6000 men were in attendance. He declared, " The misery of our widows has been the subject of frequent remark. I will therefore not detain you long by a full exposition of it. I will only make a general observation that that society which allows men to marry any number of times even up to the age of sixty, while it sternly forbids even girls of seven or eight to have another husband after one is dead; which gives liberty to a man of fifty or sixty to marry a girl of eleven or twelve, which has no word of condemnation for the man who marries another wife within fifteen days after the death of the first, is a society which sets very little value upon the life of a female human being, and places woman on the same level with cattle, and is thus in an unsound condition, disqualifying it for a successful competition with societies with a more healthy constitution. Ofttimes the marriage of a girl under certain circumstances proves her death warrant.* This matter has within the last few years forced itself powerfully upon my observation. A young man of thirty or thirty-five loses his first wife. Straightway he proceeds to marry

---

* The Professor may have had in mind the case of Phulmani Das, the girl of eight years married to a man of thirty-eight who died on the very night of her marriage. The mother in her agony over the loss of her child told a friend of the incident, and it was spread abroad throughout the community. The horror of the event caused the enactment of a law to raise the age of consent to fourteen. Against this, the priests organized public demonstrations to protest against such an interference with their religious customs.

another who is a girl of ten or twelve. That girl
dies by the time she reaches the age of twenty.
Another takes her place immediately. She too
dies similarly. Then comes a third who meets with
a same fate, and a fourth is married by the per-
severing man and is eventually left a widow before she is out of her teens. A great many such
cases have occurred within the last few years
amongst our educated men. The medical men
whom I have consulted, say that the results are
due to the marriages being ill-assorted, i. e., to the
great inequality between the ages of the girl and
the strong and vigorous man. I do not know how
else to characterize these cases, except as cases of
human sacrifice. Surely, if the men who marry
girls successively in this manner are educated men,
their refined sentiments and feelings ought to make
them spare poor, innocent girls and marry a grown
up woman, a widow, if an unmarried one is not
to be had."

The Honorable Mr. Justice Rao Bahadur M.
Ranade testifies also of his country's ideals:—" A
Hindu widow may not remarry. Against the
child-widow the rule prohibiting re-marriage is enforced with inexorable rigour. For them there is
no relaxation, no pity, no sympathy. But the old
Hindu widower, who is shuddering on the verge of
the grave may marry again and again, as often as
he likes. For him there is no restriction—he is
under no obligation to exercise self-restraint."

Ramabai knew something of the bitterness of the life of the widow, even though her Christian faith freed her from most of its trammels. It is a curious fact that even when she had become famous through the establishment of her school, when she visited in her step-brothers' home they showed affection for her, and pride in her career, but the wife would only occasionally condescend to eat in the same room with the widow. On such rare occasions Ramabai was obliged to serve herself and to wash her own dishes, while the brother and his wife, whenever they had sat by her side, or touched her hand, as they sometimes did, felt it necessary to purify themselves from the contact by changing their garments before they would venture to eat. Yet she succeeded in gaining from them a promise to send their two child-widow daughters to her school.

III

HOME-TOUCHES

AT the close of the ten year period for which the pledge of support had been made Ramabai again came to plead her cause, this time not with uncertainty as to the possibilities of success, but in order that her enlarged ideals might prevail for the future development of the work. She felt it necessary also so to change the Articles of Incorporation that no longer could they be interpreted so as to prevent her from giving Christian instruction to those who desired it. The strong conviction was that she should be as free in the exercise of her faith as she permitted those to be who preferred the Hindu customs and worship.

A large gathering came to hear her address in Channing Hall, Boston on March 16, 1898. The Pundita reported the success of the enterprise and acknowledged that she had incurred one great debt —not of money on the land or buildings; of the ninety-five thousand dollars which had been contributed during the decade fifty thousand have been given back to the Association in the value of the School, and ten thousand in the value of the

Farm,—but the truly heavy debt of gratitude for the support and the love and faith which had been so generously given. She had asked in the beginning for five thousand a year for expenses; six thousand had been sent, and for the enlarged work now possible she hoped that twenty thousand a year would not seem too much to give. Taking up the matter of the persecution which had come to the Shârada Sadan because of the conversion of certain pupils she continued: " What shall I say of the religious policy of the school? When I began my work, I told you that the school would be entirely non-sectarian. By this I did not mean that it would be an irreligious school. No kind of religious training is compulsory. We do not teach the Bible or the Vedas to the girls; but, as I told you at the beginning, I put the Bible and the Vedas together on the shelves of the library, and let the girls read for themselves if they wish. We give them all liberty to keep their castes and their customs. They are not prevented from praying to their own gods or from wearing those gods around their necks if they want to, and some of the girls in my school do so, as I used to do years ago; but I am glad to say that some light came to them, not from ourselves but from God. I was a Christian woman, I had a home, a daughter for whom I must make a home. I let my girls do what they liked, and I have the freedom with which Christ has made me free; and why should I keep my light under a bushel? When I had my family worship in my own room, not in the school hall, some of the girls began to come. Some of the Hindu brethren thought I was going too far, that I was Christianizing these girls. They wanted me to shut the door of my room when I was reading the Bible and praying. I said: 'No. I have the same freedom to practise my Christianity which those girls have to practise their religion. Why should I shut the door of my room, which I do not shut at any other time during the twenty-four hours of the day?' So the girls who want to come, come; and, though we never preached Christianity, they read the Bible for themselves." In order to remove the impression which was understood in India to bind her not to teach Christianity, the Ramabai Association was dissolved, and the property and rights were transferred to a new Association under the title of the American Ramabai Association, which still exists as the official representative of Ramabai's work in this country, and which receives and disburses the bequests and gifts which come from those who recognize that the great institution which Ramabai established must be carried on, and that her work must be finished by others, since its value is no longer a question but a proved fact.

During this visit Ramabai reported as the result of only ten years work that she had trained fourteen of the High Caste Hindu widows as teachers, nine of whom were in good positions, and two had already started schools of their own. Eight had been trained as nurses, two were housekeepers and ten happily married. Of the 350 who had been in the Shârâdâ Sadan forty-eight had become Christians—under the unconscious influence of Ramabai's daily life.

The Pundita must have suffered many hardships as she travelled through this country, from Maine to California, presenting her work and organizing Circles for its support. It requires a strong constitution to endure the constant strain of change of climate and fatigue. One minor difficulty may be related which made her achievement quite extraordinary to those who know India. What the Pundita suffered because of her strict vegetarianism will never he told, as her charming courtesy forbade her from making her distaste known, and she therefore often went without sufficient food. Many times, as we later learned, she could touch nothing on the table but the potatoes! When her preference became known the friends tried to have regard for her diet, but some most amusing experiences were hers. A luncheon arranged in her honor by a gracious hostess in New York called together many distinguished women.

Unfortunately no one had informed the lady of the house so it turned out that of the various courses every one contained some kind of flesh, so Ramabai touched only the bread and butter.

Her hostess became aware of the situation and was much distressed. When the dessert arrived she announced with glee that here was something which the guest of the day could enjoy! Upon Ramabai's return to Mukti she was describing to her girls some of the queer manners and customs of the United States. Unconscious of the fact that among her listeners was an American lady, whose sense of humor made her delight in the situation, Ramabai mentioned her occasional hunger when seated at tables loaded with plenty, and then told of that particular feast just referred to. She said that the hostess, smiling happily, urged her to partake of the dessert, a delicately browned cake heaped with rosy strawberries and covered with mounds of whipped cream! Beautiful to look at and fragrant! Ramabai was about to enjoy it when in a curious mood she inquired how it was made, and this is her report: " Fancy dear girls, what they had done! Over those luscious berries they had put a cake made with pig oil! " The word used in India for lard does not convey fully the horror which these dainty vegetarians felt on receiving such awful news, but one can imagine the shouts of laughter which followed as the students pondered their own better ways. For the pig in hot countries is an abhorrence and worse than any other kind of meat!

When Ramabai was a guest in my own home I prepared the best curry I could for her, hoping that as I had learned the art in India, also my native land, it might prove acceptable. It was easy to see however that it did not quite meet with approval. On pressing for the reason Ramabai's honesty led her to inform me that I had made three mistakes—first in using curry powder out of a bottle (though made by a leading firm) since the Brahmins never use anything but the fresh spices and peppers, secondly because I had used chicken! —and lastly because I had used onions, a low caste vegetable! We had a good laugh over all the blunders, and the next day I invited her into the kitchen to do what she pleased. I watched her as she daintily clarified the butter till it resembled the ghee used in India, to which she then added the spices and lastly the peppers. Let us hope that this one meal at least was as she desired it!

The second reception given to the brave pioneer was even more enthusiastic than on the occasion of her first visit. Ample support being assured by the American Ramabai Association, she returned to India, and with the aid of her daughter Manoramabai extended her activities marvelously. At the time of a terrible epidemic of bubonic plague during which Poona was sorely afflicted, she became convinced that quarters outside of the city were better adapted for the growing Institution, and with the assent of the Association she moved her work to a place near the village of Kedgaon, where she secured a large amount of land and erected a number of buildings, calling the whole establishment Mukti, or " Salvation," and where, during the famine, she received large numbers of widows and orphans, until her family numbered from 1500 to 2000 souls. Naturally, the form of her work changed, as in that time of need she abandoned the policy of accepting only high-caste girls. Much of the funds for the purchase of this land was sent to her from friends direct, and is not under the control of this Association. The character of her work necessarily changed. These famine-striken, neglected children and older widows were not ready for the high-school work which the pupils of the Shârada Sadan were taking, and it was therefore necessary to begin industrial work. From that time on this has been a noted feature of the great establishment. Not only is the cooking for this large number done by the girls, but the weaving of their clothing is carried on in a number of low buildings, where the cotton is carded, spun, and dyed, and then woven into the neat saris (dresses) for the large establishment. One set of girls weave in the mornings, going to school in the afternoons, while others, enjoying the morning session, keep the looms busy in the afternoons. I found it a charming sight to see the bright-colored cottons flashing in the Chakkas looms, and the swift brown hands sending the shuttle to and fro. Improved American churns have been imported for the making of butter, and

Two child-widows of India. The one at the left has been two months in the Shárada Sadan, the other Graduates of the Shárada Sadan.

Ramabai has a large farm on which vegetables
and fruit are raised for the establishment. Carpet-
making is being introduced also.

In all this work Ramabai was fortunate in having the full sympathy and coöperation of her
gifted daughter, Manoramabai, who after a course
in the Chesboro Seminary returned to India and
later completed her college course in Bombay University. The tie between mother and daughter
became one of those rare friendships that charm
the onlooker. Mano existed only for the joy of
helping her mother and to fulfill her plans. Ramabai in turn so trusted Mano that she gave to her
the administration of the Shâradâ Sadan, and indeed, the oversight of the school work, while she
devoted her attention to the general administration,
for the various departments coming out of the
famine conditions required generalship to keep all
at work and all happy and healthy. In later years
the routine of necessity became very exact. We
are fortunate to have Ramabai's own description
of her day's work: " The big church bell rang at
4 a. m., to rouse everybody from sleep. I was up.
At 4:30 I walked out of my room to the church,
where I saw the pupil teachers and some of the
new girls assembled for prayer and Bible study.
They sang a hymn after which I read the Bible lesson and explained. Prayers were offered, and the
meeting was closed with the Lord's Prayer. It is

6:15 a.m.   The pupil teachers have gone to take their breakfast, and to prepare for school.   All of us workers, too, have to take our breakfast at this time,   The new girls rose at 5 a.m.: their matrons helped them to put their bedding in good order and to sweep the sleeping rooms.   The girls who do the washing for the little girls and for the invalids have tied up their bundles of clothes, taken them up, and placed them on their heads.   Water is drawn from the well in large leather buckets.   Four pair of bullocks and three men are helping to draw it.   The water is poured into two tanks, whence it flows into the garden to water the fruit, plants, and vegetables.   Here in these tanks all the washing is done in the morning, and the clothes are dried in the sun.   Some of the girls gather up the clothes, and, after taking their bath and washing their saris, the washerwomen return home at about eleven o'clock, take their mid-day meal, and go to school.

"The pupil teachers, after breakfast, go to school.   At 8 a.m., some classes of the Rescue Home girls come to the school-room to learn their lessons till 10 a.m., and go to bathe.   The large girls of the Mukti Home have gone to have their bath while the little girls were having their breakfast.   Now it is their turn to have their breakfast while the smaller girls are having their bath.   One of the older girls, who is a teacher now, is going

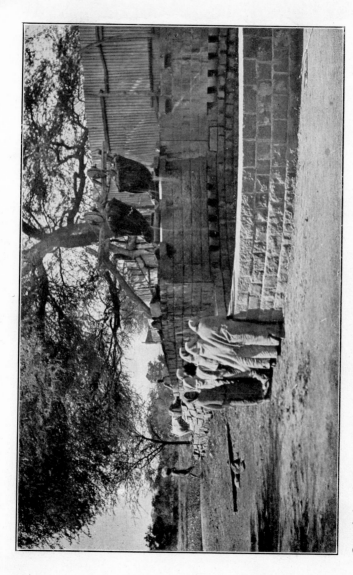

One of the nine great wells at Mukti. The water supply has never failed. Bullocks pull up the water in the skin buckets.

around the grounds watching the sanitary conditions, directing the sweepers how to keep the place clean. She also goes around the dormitories and sees that the bedding, etc., of the girls in each class is kept in good order. It is her duty to report to me if the general cleanliness of the establishment is neglected.

" I walked around the place, saw the workmen engaged in the work at the proper places, directed the foreman to make certain improvements in some places, to dig the foundation of a new room to be built near the lamp room, directed the gardener to plant trees in one part of the ground and to take out some trees, which came too near the building, and plant them in another place. Went to inspect the hospital grounds. At 10 a.m. the pupil teachers have finished their morning lessons. They rise from their desks to make room for the other girls, there not being room for all at one time, and a host of new girls of all sizes are seen going to the school-room. In ten minutes they are seated in their proper places, slates and pencils have been distributed, the blackboards are before them, and the teachers have begun a fresh lesson. The kindergarten department has begun its interesting work. The head girl who directs the pupil teachers in this department is in a bad temper, and has left her work abruptly, so it falls to my share to go and teach in the kindergarten to-day. The children are learning the Third Gift. The bell is ringing. The morning session of the school has come to a close, and the girls are going out of the school-rooms to have their mid-day meal. The new girls are gathering again in their respective classes to have another two hours' instruction. The pupil teachers have gone to their study in the school-room. Some classes from among the new girls have gone to grind grain to make flour for bread. About sixty hand-mills, in two large grinding-rooms, are being worked at.

" At 3 P. M. the bell rings for all the girls to come together in church, to attend the singing class. They come from all sides with their matrons. The little ones and middle-sized girls are most anxious to learn singing. At 4 p.m. the girls go out of the singing class to their rooms, take their platter, cups, etc., go to the tank to wash their hands and take water in their drinking vessels, and go to the dining-rooms, where they are led by the matrons in the proper order. When the chief matron rings a small bell to call order and to say grace, all girls stand, fold their hands, bend their heads reverently, and ask God's blessing. Supper is over at 6 p.m., and they have a little time for play. Some are walking about, some sitting in the open ground, some dancing and singing and enjoying themselves. Some chat in the garden, and inspect flowers and leaves. They are beginning to love flowers. A year ago they used to tear up the leaves of the flower plants and break the branches of the growing trees.

" Night has come. The bell for retiring is ringing. The girls hurry off from the garden to their respective dormitories. Each one spreads her bedding of a little carpet, a sheet, and two blankets. They are preparing to lie down and go off to sleep. But before going to bed they kneel down, either by themselves or around their matrons, and pray aloud. These new girls, babes in Christ, are just beginning to understand what praying means. Their expressions are very funny at times. They mean well. Some wee babes who are beginning to lisp are repeating just one verse from the twenty-third Psalm over and over again, ' The Lord is my Shepherd. I shall NOT W-A-A-ANT.' Great stress is laid on the last two words. The poor little things have known too well what want means. At eight the bell rings again, when all the girls are in bed."

The institution was divided into three parts,— Mukti, or the general Orphanage or School for all who may come; Kripa Sadan, or the Home of Refuge, for those whose lives have been unsheltered before they came to her; and the Shârada Sadan, or the high-school department, which was kept quite separate from the others and which is the institution which the American Association supports. In this to-day there are two hundred and four students, and the teachers are wholly those trained in the institution. From these institutions have gone out teachers to other schools in many parts of India. Another occasion for rejoicing is that many of these young women, coming as child-widows, having been educated and their characters built up into beautiful womanliness, have since been married and are making happy homes for themselves. Some, indeed are attempting to carry out Ramabai's plans by inaugurating similar institutions on a small scale, one in the city of Poona being conducted on strictly Hindu lines with caste rules and regulations.

A school for the blind is one of the features of the establishment; and, as Ramabai's great heart never refused the afflicted, and deaf and dumb have also found an asylum under her loving care. It is impossible to tell what was the power of this little woman to attract the love and obedience of the hundreds of daughters. One can only say that she was endowed with the gift of loving and, therefore, of being loved. Her work has not been confined to what has been done within the walls of Mukti. The people of India have been compelled to change their views on the subject of the education of women within the last twenty-five years, and the success of Ramabai's work has been a very large factor in this change. She used to relate the story of a prince who visited her to reproach her for abjuring the faith of her fathers. The sight of the happy children seemed to arouse the ire of his highness, but he voiced the feelings of many when he contemptuously exclaimed: "A school for widows! What right have they to have happiness or education? Those who have no husbands or sons to serve are of no more value than the street dogs and crows, and might as well live like them. They can easily get a grain of bread and a handful of rice to subsist upon."

It is a sad pity that the answer to this is not recorded, for with her keen mind and wit there must have been some scathing truth presented to his Highness!

IV

LIFE STORIES

THE stories of some of the students in the Shâradâ Sadan are absorbing. Many have appeared in the Annual Reports of the Association. Manorama made a trip to the United States in 1890, and spoke at the Annual Meeting of the Association, giving the following incidents.

" I would like to tell of the lives of some of our girls who have afterwards proved to be most useful helpers. One was married when she was five years old to a man of forty-five and she became a widow when she was six. Then she lived with her husband's brother who kept a country inn in Central India. As the child grew up she had to do much of the work of the house. When not more than ten she was obliged, besides all the other work, to go to a well about a quarter of a mile from the house a number of times a day to bring water in the copper jars. She carried one on her head, one on her hip and one in her hand. Then she had to wait on the guests who came to the inn, and sometimes when she had gone to bed at eleven she would have to get up because guests had come. She must get warm water for them to wash their feet, and make them comfortable. Her life was perfect misery. She tried to run away, but she did not know the country, and all she could do was to run a little way and sit down on the roadside and cry until people found her and took her home to be beaten cruelly. At last somebody took pity on her and she was brought to our school. She remained about seven years and got an education sufficient to make her self supporting. She has been married to a native Christian man and is very happy. She and her husband are trying to do all they can for their people. Her own idea is to help little widows.

Then T., a fine scholar, came from South India. She knows many languages, two of the dialects of the places where she lived, and she had to learn Marathi. Then she studies Sanscrit and English, and now takes Latin. She was married when only eight, but says that the only time she remembers seeing her husband was at the marriage. She intends to open a school for widows.

Y. was married when quite young and lived in an orthodox Hindu family. Her brother brought his wife to our school, but would not bring Y. because she was a widow. One of her duties was to go every morning to get water from a well. About the same time a man living next door started for business. In India it is considered unlucky for a widow to cross one's path, the work of the whole day is undone by it. So the man complained and said he would not allow it. One incident which she told of her life is a bit amusing. A widow is supposed to fast regularly once a week, and once a month she fasts so strictly that she is not allowed even to drink a drop of water. When the time comes for her to take her first meal she is allowed only to eat bread made of a certain kind of flour. Y. had been fasting this way and when it was time for her to eat she asked her sister-in-law for some of the flour. The answer was that there was no flour of the kind in the house. Y. begged for she was very hungry but the sister-in-law after making a feint of searching said there was no flour. According to Hindu philosophy a man must not speak what is not true, but there are five cases in which he may tell a lie. One of these is that he may say what is not true to a woman. The next day Y. found a large sack of this particular flour and could not understand why her sister-in-law should have said this, but supposed it was a matter of religion and therefore all right. Later she came to our school and is so much touched by the kind way in which she is treated that she says she cannot understand why you are so kind to a widow."

" J. is the girl who wants to learn everything. Her head had been shaven and she had been disfigured in many ways so that she looked miserable. When I saw her again after my absence of some months I did not know her. She had long beautiful hair and was a very pretty girl, and so happy that I did not recognize her. One day somebody said to her, " J. are you not tired? " " No, I no tired, I praising God." That is what keeps her happy.

Touched with compassion for the widows who were kept in the Shrine city of Brindaban, the reputed birthplace of Krishna, Ramabai, accompanied by a friend, went to see the conditions, Priests met them at the station, and choosing one as guide to find them shelter for the night, they were taken to a small dirty room where without food they waited for the dawn. As soon as light appeared they attempted to bathe in the river Jumna, but its sacred waters that cleanse the soul of all sin appeared to them as too filthy for their bodies. Its banks were covered with dunghills and the streets and alleys filled with intolerable odors. For two weeks the Pundita lived in this center of Hindusim going in and out, suspected because she did not visit the temples and offer worship to the many gods, but, protected by the mendicant's dress, she attempted to rescue some of the hundreds of widows. The younger widows were taught that the life of sin was pleasing to the god Krishna and that service in the temple would lead to a life of happiness hereafter. Those who resist are left to care for themselves as best they may. Some starve to death, many commit suicide. No wonder that Ramabai exclaimed, " Oh the sin and misery of it all! The heartless cruelty of man to woman which I saw on every side is beyond description. I thought I had seen the Sodom and Gomorrah of the old times and I wondered at the long suffering of God."

Seven of the widows would have been glad to leave and accompany Ramabai, but their plans were discovered and they were placed under lock and key by the priests. One only could be rescued, and the strain of the experience almost cost the life of the heroic Pandita!

As a high-caste woman, as previously stated, Ramabai was a strict vegetarian and continued the practice after her Christian ideals had liberated her from the enforcement of this. By preference she avoided meat and even eggs, using milk, the fruits of vine and field. Her skill in cookery made her menus for the students very attractive and wholesome. An American visitor described the domestic arrangements : " Go with me into the dining room and see the girls at breakfast. On each side of the room is a row of ' plats,' square pieces of wood, well finished, having a knob at each corner to raise it slightly from the floor. On each of these a pupil is seated on one side of the room. On the other side sits Ramabai and the teachers. On the floor in front of each a brass plate and bowl are placed.

One of the girls appointed to serve at this meal drops a spoonful of fried vegetables on the plate, another follows with boiled rice, a third with vegetable curry and a fourth with a teaspoonful of melted butter. These are dextrously mixed by even the youngest child. Then rice with sour buttermilk is served and unleavened bread with melted butter. Milk is given to all who desire, the children and the delicate girls having an extra quantity. This is the diet morning, noon and night year in and year out, except that at tiffin the variety is less. On holidays there is a treat of fruit and very simple sweetmeats. . . . Everything in the dining room is as neat and orderly as it is simple. Into the kitchen we cannot enter; it would be profanation (to the high caste workers therein). But into the dormitories and sick wards we may look and shall find there neatness, order and good ventilation."

The first student to come to Ramabai was little Godubai, who had twice resolved to put an end to her unhappy life, but was restrained by the fear of being born again *a woman!* Four years of Ramabai's influence and the joyous life of the Shâradâ Sadan and she was married to Mr. D. K. Karvé, and together they established a work for child-widows on the lines learned at the Sadan. A letter from Mr. Karvé is so clear that we quote briefly:

" It is not easy to mention all the numerous advantages which my wife derived from her stay

of four years at the Sadana. She has come out of
it with a keen love of knowledge and a mind enlarged and enlightened. In the time she was there
she learned Marathi up to the fifth standard and
English up to the third standard. This instruction is in the first place highly useful to her, and
secondly it has filled her with a desire to learn
more, a desire which I am doing all in my power
to gratify. Her views about life and our work in
this world have also been materially altered. She
has become free from many of our degrading su-
perstitions. She feels that she has been raised
to a sphere where she can render good work for
her more unfortunate sisters; and life seems now
a blessing instead of a curse. I find that she is
an excellent housewife. The habits of neatness
and order which she acquired in the Sadana are of
great use in managing our domestic affairs. In
short, I find her to be an excellent wife and an
excellent companion in life, and feel sure that in her
company in the natural course of things many
happy days are in store for me."

Manoramabai at all times manifested a sympathy with the students of the Sadan. She writes:
"Soon after the World War broke out a request
was made by Lady Wimbledon to the women of
Bombay Province that they should help her in
doing as much as possible for the relief of wounded
soldiers. The students in the Shâradâ Sadan were
keenly interested in the progress of the war.

Manoramabai—Heart's Joy

Many were sufficiently educated to understand the situation and they talked and prayed about current events. This in an American home might not have been surprising, but in an Indian home of thirty years ago it would have been an almost unheard of thing for women to engage intelligently in such a conversation." Mano continues:

" We have blind girls, and for some time I have been feeling that I could do better work in this department if I could have someone to help me. A lady has come from England who has had training in a Blind School.... We are trying to start a silk industry. My mother has planted a number of mulberry trees and castor oil plants, and we have a number of worms spinning their coccoons in baskets made by our girls.

" During the last hot weather vacation, I took a party of 15 to Mahableshwar for a few days. Living as we do here in this village away from the city with its civilization and all its modern improvements, we sometimes find it difficult to explain to our girls the books which they read, because their ideas of many things are so vague. For instance, some have never seen the sea, some do not remember ever being in a train, some have never seen a river or a waterfall or a high mountain; a telephone, an electric lamp, a tramcar, an elevator, a large English shop, and many other things are to them things only in name, and we find that the easiest way to explain them is by taking parties of girls to Bombay or to some other place of interest where they will be able to see things for themselves. There is an old fort in Gulbarga which is an object of great interest. I often take one or two girls with me when I go there and let them study the place. We had a good laugh once in Bombay when a girl about eighteen years old who was preparing for her College Entrance examination saw the sea for the first time and drank some of its water, forgetting that it would be salt. She had read about it but had forgotten!"

V

SCHOLAR, SAINT, SERVANT.

YES, the order is right. The distinguished woman whose life is here briefly portrayed was first a scholar of no mean achievement, master of seven languages, with more than two thousand verses of the Vedas at the command of her wonderful memory, giving public addresses in English as well as to audiences in the vernaculars of India—acclaimed Sarasvati—yes, scholar is her first title and well deserved!

Saint? Yes, also, for unembittered by the sore trial of her girlhood by the loss of all that life held dear in the way of family ties, purified by the limitations which the religious customs of her land placed upon her, and seeing through the mist of Hindu ideals the true God to whom her father directed his prayers! Saintly in character then and developed as she found the Christ who is the propitiation for the sin of the whole world.

Servant—verily! For did she not put aside thought of worldly promotion and gain that she might place her hands under the burden of the hoary centuries of oppression of the child-widows and later the starving and the afflicted. "I am

among you as one that serveth," was the word of
her Master, and she followed Him. Against the
ideal of doing good by renunciation and austerity
for the sake of laying up merit for her future, she
served for the sake of the One whose life and example met all the needs of her own heart, and
whose love encompasses the entire race of men.
" I am among you as he that serveth," said her
Christ. Following Him and Him alone she was
definitely led into the path of service—a unique
service, as Dr. Edward Everett Hale said in an
address to the Association: " Ramabai dedicated
herself to this work as Luther dedicated himself to
the reformation of the church, so that she will stand
out in history as one of those remarkable persons
taking a hand in particular work.

" General Armstrong, perhaps the greatest edu-
cator of his generation in this country, always said
that the business of the Hampton Institute was to
create a class among the blacks—a class of people
every man and woman of which shall be interested
in the education of the blacks. This little woman is
creating a class of women in India every blessed
one of whom shall be interested in the education of
child-widows."

At the beginning of her work Ramabai was accustomed to say that she could have both the Bible
and the Veda on the shelves of her school and
pupils might read what they chose. Later the Bible
became more and more the guide of the daily liv-

ing of the Mukti schools, but from choice, not compulsion.

Ramabai's high reputation as a Sanscrit scholar gave her rare opportunities. When on the occasion of the first meeting of the National Congress in Bombay in 1889 among the two thousand delegates were three women, largely because of the Pundita's influence. This national congress was convened for the purpose of the spirit of unity among the diverse races of Hindustan and for calling the attention of the British Government to existing grievances and needed reforms. Ramabai spoke forcibly on two resolutions passed, one relating to marriage and the other to the shaving of the head of the widow. She dwelt on the injustice of depriving the widow of her property if she married again. With her usual courage she denounced as a wild superstition the belief that if the widows wore their hair long it would serve to bind their husbands in hell, and asked the men how they would like to have their heads shaved because of the death of a wife! When she arose to speak there was much crowding and pushing among the men who desired to hear her. After quiet was restored she naïvely remarked, " It is not strange, my countrymen, that my voice is small, for you have never given a woman the chance to make her voice strong!" She then rushed along in a rapid talk, moving her audience to laughter and tears. The resolutions she thus supported were carried by a large majority, and the request that the members of the Conference pledge themselves not to allow marriage until the bride had completed her fourteenth year was also carried by a large majority.

Her action at this Conference created such interest that she received invitations to lecture in distant cities. She therefore made a long tour speaking on education and with direct reference to the child widow problem.

It is gratifying to note that some Hindus were liberal enough to recognize her scholarship even after she became a Christian. At Barsi she was invited to lecture and a meeting was arranged in a hall—but the women did not dare to come. The men then urged her to read for them the Hindu sacred books. She said, with characteristic frankness—" All right, I have, like Paul of old, to be a Jew for the Jews and a Greek for the Greeks!" Selecting a portion of one of the Puranas she read and explained to the crowd of men and the few women, and so delighted were the auditors that arrangements were immediately made for this ": semi-religious " lecture to be repeated that afternoon in the temple. Ramabai's sense of the ludicrous came to her aid here as in many other occasions—she wrote, " Here was the climax! Nobody had ever seen or heard of the orthodox Hindu letting a Christian outcast enter his sacred temple! The people of Barsi not only allowed me to go to their temple but besought me to go and read a portion

of their sacred book! I thought this a nineteenth
century miracle." So wise was the Pundita in
the use of the opportunity that the women pressed
her to stay longer with them.

It is encouraging to find that many enlightened
people among those of Hindu faith did welcome
this apostle of a brighter day. A Madras paper
thus characterized the distinguished visitor to that
city " Pundita Ramabai combines in herself what
even in men in India is rare:—a deep knowledge
of the Hindu Shastras and also an intimate ac-
quaintance with the life, thought and speech of the
most advanced nations of the West. For several
centuries a lady Sanyasi so learned and so devoted
to the elevation of her sex as Ramabai has not
appeared on the stage of Indian life. In spite of
her conversion to Christianity the simple and un-
ostentatious life she is at present leading, her earnest eloquence in a sacred cause, and the invincible
front she presents to orthodoxy by her citations
from the Vedas and Puranas, would in any other
country but India, in any other age but the present one of extreme selfishness, have sufficed to
create a moral and social revolution; but even in
the degenerate times in which our lot is cast, we
are hopeful that the pleadings of the Pundita will
remind our educated men of their duty to women-
kind."

In other cities Ramabai was received with
high honors, feted, and garlanded with flowers,

and sprinkled with perfumed water. It was the
answer to the centuries of mute protest of India's
women against inhuman cruelty,—the protest
that was at last voiced in the eloquent life of
one heroic woman, who gathered the miseries of
her sisters into her own heart and turned them
into the sweetness of hope and the strength of
prophecy.

The Editor of the Bombay Educational Record
published the following: " If the election of Mr.
Nauroji to Parliament was a romantic incident,
as *The Times* says, what epithet, we wonder, should
be applied to the journey to America of an unpro-
tected Hindu widow, to her loving reception by
American ladies, to the formation of Ramabai
Circles, to the return of the wanderer to India, but
with links binding her to America, and finally to
the installation a few days ago of a Shâradâ Sadan
in a building of its own with an assured income,
that will enable it to carry on its beneficent work.
Romantic is no word for it! It is gratifying to
know that all that is best in native society is in
hearty sympathy with the work of the gifted and
brave Maratha lady. The race which can produce
such a woman certainly need to dispair of nothing,
and the whole pathetic story, so creditable as it is
to America, gives one quite a new conception of the
possibilities which seem to lie in the future from
the increasing recognition of the solidarity of man-
kind." The utterances of the Subodha Patrika

The Chapel and School House at Mukti.

are yet more significant. " The history of Pundita Ramabai School may well deserve to be written in characters of gold. It is a Hindu woman's pluck which brought it into existence and it is American generosity which supports it."

Even the task of guiding the lives of her immense family, of directing the industries, farm work, printing, weaving, etc., in which every girl was trained unless she was found to be especially well adapted to the teaching profession, was not enough for this great hearted leader. She looked beyond the walls of her mission upon the needy folk of her race, the Marathi people. The ordinary villager was not able to understand the language of the translation of the Bible as it is in the classical Marathi, so well adapted to the demands of the educated, so she determined to give the people a translation in the vulgate—the every day speech of the villagers. In order to understand perfectly the meaning of the original she spent some years in preparing an interlinear translation of five different versions of the words and idioms of the Old Testament, and her preparation was as thorough for the New. To supplement her own knowledge of Greek and Hebrew she had several students make a special study of each language and with these set herself to her great task. All the printing required was done by the girls in the press at Mukti; and when one thinks of the multifarious characters, Roman, Marathi, Greek and Hebrew

type used in the typesetting, the greatness of the
achievement becomes almost incredible.   Not
seventy translators, but Ramabai alone with her
students made this version!   And she did it well!
The support of her beloved daughter Manoramabai
made possible the leisure necessary for this
task.   After Mano had finished her course in Bombay University she took entire charge of the school
work in the various departments, and with the aid
of teachers raised almost entirely from the institution brought the work of the Shâradâ Sadan up to
Government requirements—a course somewhat like
that of our American High School.

Intensely loyal to her own land and people,
Ramabai had the national spirit; but she recognized that only by taking the best of all the world's
store of learning and gifts could India be restored
to its former greatness. At first she steadfastly refused to accept Government aid for her school, in
the belief that she would be more free if she did
not attempt to comply with the conditions laid
down by the Educational Laws. But after almost
twenty years she became convinced that these plans
were really best for the educational development of
the people, so she adapted her work to the Government conditions and recognized their efforts made
for the intellectual elevation of her country. The
idea of keeping living conditions simple in order
that the burden of poorer people might not be
made heavier was always paramount in her mind.

The looms in her institution were the " chakkas " of the village, the oil presses were such as used by the people, the farm work was carried on with native tools except where she recognized the superior advantage of foreign implements for increasing the yield of the fields; her students worked in the printing office and on the presses, learning not only the lighter tasks, but how to care for the mechanical equipment, being taught by expert machinists. The growth of the settlement around Mukti soon entitled it to be recognized as a village, and Ramabai was appointed " Lambadar," the official head.

In 1919 the British Government awarded to Pundita Ramabai the Kaiser-I-Hind medal for distinguished service to Indian education. The value to the country of her initiative in providing for the lessening of economic waste by her demonstration that the millions of widows might be educated and thus made valuable to the community, instead of being a burden to the family and a blight on the nation, was thus fitly recognized. Ramabai's health at the time did not permit her to go to Bombay for the ceremony of conferring this high honor, so Manoramabai received it for her.

Manoramabai extended the influence of the Shâradâ Sadan by establishing, about eight years ago, another school at Gulbarga, in the Nizam's dominions, which has done fine work, the daughters of leading men of the region being enrolled. Other schools have sprung up in different parts of India, which owe their initiative directly to Ramabai's influence; of these some are not Christian, but they are working for the elevation of the widows and thus carrying on her ideals.

Mano's activities in other directions were manifold. With a companion she made trips to Australia and New Zealand, presenting the work with great acceptability, and Circles formed under this inspiration have contributed generously to the support of the Shâradâ Sadan.

In 1920 the building held by the Association in Poona was sold for seventy-two thousand Rupees, of which twelve thousand was placed in Ramabai's hands and sixty thousand invested in India under the care of Dr. R. A. Hume, the representative of the Association, for the support of the Shâradâ Sadan, for this institution must continue its work, and funds will still be needed from the friends who believe in the value of education for India's women.

All plans of the Association as well as those of Ramabai looked towards the continuance of the work under the direction of her gifted daughter, Manoramabai. Heart's Joy she had in every deed proven herself to be, taking from her mother the strain of every possible duty she could perform, working in fullest sympathy and with marked success. However, God's plan was different. Her failing health had for some time been a cause of anxiety, and in spite of the most tender care given at the Hospital at Miraj, her constitution was unable to sustain the burden of work which she had so bravely carried. An operation was resorted to, but her heart was not equal to the strain and she went quietly to the heavenly country towards which her thoughts and love had constantly turned. The stricken mother was noble in this affliction, which meant indescribable loss to her work as well as to her loving heart. She wrote to the officers of the Association " Let me thank you for your loving sympathy. All I have to say is ' The Lord gave and the Lord has taken away, Blessed be the name of the Lord.'

" There are 360 pupils studying in the Shâradâ Sadan, the Primary and the Kindergarten. This work shall be continued as long as God gives us grace and strength. The school was well organized and brought to its present state by my daughter, who has gone to the next world before me! One of her last acts was to make the time tables for the school before it recommenced in June. She attended the meeting of the Trustees and spoke and arranged for the next meeting to be held shortly, saying that though she would not be here to attend the session as she was going to the hospital; but all the business would be carried on in due order, as she had arranged for everything." These words were almost prophetic, for Manoramabai passed into the presence of the King before the next meeting took place.

Though the bereaved mother carried her grief so courageously, the effect of the sorrow, however bravely borne, and the loss of the support which Mano had so unfailingly given, proved too much for a constitution which, strong in the beginning, had been enfeebled by the rigors of her many pilgrimages and the austerities of her early life. Soon after sending to the Association the Annual Report of the Shârada Sadan she quietly appointed as her successor Miss Lissa Hastie, an English friend who had worked with her for the past twelve years and who is in full sympathy with her ideals. On April 5th came the cable which announced " Ramabai Promoted."

Yes, promoted to the service above! What a welcome from the thousands whose lives she had touched with blessings—the little ones, the famine stricken, the blind and the leper; all these had received ministry from her hands.

The funeral service was conducted by Rev. R. A. Hume, of Amednagar, the representative of the Association in India, and a life long friend of Ramabai's, assisted by Rev. W. W. Bruere, acting pastor at Mukti. The simple casket was carried on the shoulders of the young women of Mukti, and the thousand students of Mukti followed to the village cemetery a quarter of a mile distant. Over the coffin was a white cloth on which was inscribed, " We shall all be changed, the trumpet shall sound and the dead shall be raised incorruptible, and we shall be changed." On the cover of the casket was the inscription " The Pundita Ramabai Medhavi—born April 23, 1858; slept April 5, 1922."

Remarkable was the self control of those who might naturally have been expected to indulge in the Oriental emotional excess, instead of which there was notable effort at self control, and while there were occasional outbreaks of crying it was evident that the faith and the teachings of the beloved mother had impressed upon them the lesson of the rising again to blessed immortality.

This remarkable woman had held her mind open to new truths, and therefore was sometimes in danger of being influenced by some who held extreme views. From this danger her characteristic common sense released her, and, without adopting any special creed, her Christianity was of that type which embraces with warm affection every other follower of her Lord and King. The very breath of her being was for the Master, and her motto of life " Others," was the index of her wide affection. The name she gave to her mission was Mukti—Salvation—and the deep spiritual life which was manifest in the daily program cannot be forgotten by those who have been privileged to witness it. The effect of the voices of fifteen hundred girls and women united in vocal prayer, each asking for the needs of their own hearts without attention to those about them, was a unique ex-

perience, and one which called for no criticism of
the apparent confusion of sound, but a questioning
as to the effect which such earnestness had on the
hearts of those who could shut out self and com-
mune with their Father in Heaven. India has
much to teach to us of the more self-conscious
western world.

Though unable to hear the religious services,
Ramabai was always present if health permitted,
and the very sight of the white robed figure seated
in prayer and meditation was a benediction to all
her family as well as to the visitors to Mukti, who
came from all lands of the earth to witness and
marvel at the work of one woman's hands and
mind. Yet with all she was very human, and her
extraordinary executive ability which kept everything moving in perfect order and harmony did not
make her stern and unlovely.

Miss Fuller, one of her younger associates at
Mukti, gives this charming picture of the beloved
leader: " She was a heroine even to her daily helpers. She was one of the finest types of the Kon-
kansth Brahmins, finely organized, very keen in
all her senses until she became deaf as a result
of sleeping on damp earth during her pilgrimages
before she became a Christian. Not much over
five feet in height, small boned and very shapely,
with a remarkable presence, beautiful for its unconscious dignity and modesty. She always wore
white cotton *saris,* token of her widowhood (her

hair short for the same reason). Her little feet that had walked over four thousand miles on pilgrimages were our delight. Whatever she did she did with delicate accuracy, grace and charm. Whether she corrected proofs, or fed a baby, or listened to a bore, she was exquisite. Her name means " Delight " with the double sense of Delight-Giver or Delight-Filled, and her faculty for enjoyment was one of the proofs of her humanness. Her sense of humour was a quenchless fountain and she had the most infectious laugh! I have been told that years ago when she was with a certain very entertaining friend they would both laugh until they could no longer sit up. One might be very bold with her if one were humorous. If one told her she was wonderful, one was gravely suppressed. But once when I remarked on her cleverness, using an idiom with two meanings, she promptly chose the unflattering sense and shook with laughter. She could be very droll. When she was too ill to talk much, she would send us into fits of laughter sometimes with one absurd gesture—made with the utmost dignity of her delicate hands. Bai was always doing thoughtful pretty things, and I have never in this world known anyone so generous, so big-hearted, so lavish-hearted. She was almost constitutionally incapable of selling anything. With the exception of the great joy she always had in telling her countrymen of her adored Saviour and Master Jesus

Christ, in seeing any of them find Him, and in translating, printing on her own presses and giving out (gratis always) the Bible or portions of it, there was nothing which gave her so much pleasure as giving. Doubtless her own experiences of hunger in famine time deepened the satisfaction she felt in satisfying hunger in others. She simply could not understand meanness and selfishness."

She loved children and children went to her as needles to a magnet. Many a baby at Mukti, some of them now half-grown, has been fed and bathed with her own hands, not occasionally, but week in and week out. And many a girl and woman could boast that " Sarasvatidevi " had sponged and rubbed her down in fever and sent her tidbits from her own plate. Bai has written a little song for children about two of her cats who used to quarrel because one of them would nurse the other's kitten and its own proper mother objected. She wrote many other such songs for Muldnyana, the primer she wrote and published for village children. She took six months from her Bible translation to write the poetry, the reading lessons and other matter in that splendid little book. No wonder it is so popular. It is the only one of her publications which she ever sold, as she had strong prejudices against selling the Word of God. The lessons in the primer are a connected story of the Gospel, but not in the actual

words of the Bible. When I once remarked to
a young Brahman visitor how unusual it was for
a mind packed with such solid knowledge and great
learning as hers to be able to write such pretty
and even nonsensical songs for children as the
primer contains, he said that when a door was
so large, small things could go through as easily
as big ones, which I thought a delightful answer.
It was that remarkable combination of great ad-
ministrative ability and faculty for minute de-
tail, which in conjunction with her great confi-
dence in God enabled her to do so much and so
many different kinds of things. Max Muller said
she had one of the most remarkable memories in
the world, and of that we had daily proof to the
very end.

Bai was never too busy to be courteous. Few
things displeased her more than rudeness or un-
couthness in those who should know better; and
if her own specially trained elder girls failed in
good manners to a guest she was grieved to the
heart. She was gracious without effusion. Her
fine breeding showed constantly in the simplicity
of her manners and speech. She never flattered,
and one could count on her for a sincere opinion.
She would suffer much discomfort rather than
hurt anyone's feelings, and I have heard her sigh
softly for wasted time and aching head after listen-
ing to volubility hold forth on emptiness. However, when there was need she could dismiss people

so beautifully that they scarcely knew themselves how the tide of their enthralling discourse had been stemmed.

Another most evident trait of Bai's character was her profoundly sincere and lovely humility. It did not consist of making modest speeches or abasing herself—nor was she secretly warmed by praise. No one who knew her could doubt the genuineness of her dislike of adulation. She has been known to get up and go suddenly to her room —as one involuntarily leaves a suffocating room —when the talk turned on herself.

" I suppose the secret of her bigness, of her glorious humility, of her power, was that she was so wholly given to God, so sold to His will, so utterly and joyously the bondservant of the Lord Jesus Christ, that there was left in her no room for self. She wanted nothing for herself—not merely was she free from the desire of money and things, but from any personal ambition, from any craving for fame, or even the love, appreciation and thanks of those she served. With all her heart she wanted that God be glorified in all things and that His Kingdom come. She never tried to attract anyone; one felt she would not raise a finger to attach one to herself. It did not come into her mind. She only wanted those who worked with her to work for God's glory as she did. To her it was an honor and privilege to serve Him at Mukti. She had herself deliberately laid aside a

great and unique career for the joy of serving
her Master's brethren, whether greater, lesser or
least, she did not care. To her it was a joy—
high, solemn, heart-lifting joy; and there was no
choice at all between service at Mukti and some
lucrative post, a professional career or mere marriage. These were only commonplaces. I have
heard her say that if millions of Hindu widows
could live celibate, just because custom forbade
them remarriage—even though the first marriage
had been only nominal—surely it was no great
thing for Christian women to give up marriage
for the service of the needy, the afflicted, the
destitute, and for the bringing in of the Kingdom
of God. Can the ocean understand the pond?
And is it strange if the pond sometimes wistfully
thought the ocean a little unfeeling? And it was
because she did not seek love that it flowed to her
as rivers to the sea. She inspired the tenderest
devotion, the blindest faith, the maddest loyalty.
It was curious—and yet not really so—that she
should have been kissed so much when she was
so unresponsive to merely emotional demonstration. I have seen American and European men
visitors kiss her hand as though she were a queen-
mother, while for me the dab of cream of top of
all was the delectable fact that I was kissing the
Pandita Ramabai Dongre Medhavi, acclaimed
Sarasvati (Goddess of Wisdom) herself by the
assembled pundits of Calcutta, greater altogether

than her great international reputation, and one of the best and sweetest women that ever lived."

This tender tribute is well deserved. We who know Ramabai from her first visit to the United States can testify to her absolute unselfish nature, and her rare gifts. Dr. Fleming, in " Building With India," speaks for us who knew her intimately:—" In the history of the Christian Church Pundita Ramabai will stand out as the greatest Indian Christian of her generation. In her long toilsome pilgrimages, in her arduous search through the entire range of Sanscrit literature for some satisfying truth, the Church will see the impotence of Hinduism taken at its highest. In her remarkable combination of executive, intellectual and religious powers, in her great work for thousands of India's widows, in her unhesitating loyalty to Jesus Christ and her humble service for Him, in what she was, even more than what she has done, the world may see what an India soul may be when possessed by Christ!"

THE AMERICAN RAMABAI
ASSOCIATION

President
MRS. ARTHUR PERRY, Boston.

Vice-Presidents
REV. HARLAN P. BEACH, D.D., New Haven.
REV. LYMAN ABBOTT, D.D., New York.
REV. D. D. ADDISON, D.D., Brookline.
REV. GEORGE A. GORDON, D.D., Boston.
REV. ALEXANDER MANN, D.D., Boston.

Treasurer
MR. EDGAR C. LINN, 1318 Beacon St., Brookline, Mass.

Corresponding Secretary
MISS CLEMENTINA BUTLER,
Wesleyan Building, Boston.

Recording Secretary
MISS ALICE H. BALDWIN,
233 Fisher Ave., Brookline.

Managers
MISS CLEMENTINA BUTLER.
MISS ANNA H. CHACE.
MRS. E. C. E. DORION.
MISS ANTOINETTE P. GRANGER.
MRS. C. O. DORCHESTER.
MR. A. M. FRITCHLEY.

MISS S. B. RICH.
MR. HENRY FAIRBANKS.
MRS. THEODORE S. LEE.
MRS. JAMES McKEEN.
MRS. S. W. LEE-MORTIMER.
MRS. HENRY W. PEABODY.
MRS. ARTHUR PERRY.
JULIA MORTON PLUMMER, M.D.
ARTHUR K. STONE, M.D.
MRS. W. H. THURBER.
REV. ROBERT A. HUME, D.D.
                    (Ahmednagar, India).

Executive Committee

MISS CLEMENTINA BUTLER, Chairman,
                    Wesleyan Bldg., Boston.
MISS ANNA H. CHACE, Providence, R. I.
MRS. C. O. DORCHESTER, West Newton, Mass.
MRS. HENRY W. PEABODY, Beverly, Mass.
MRS. T. S. LEE, Boston, Mass.
MRS. S. W. LEE-MORTIMER, Boston, Mass.

Principal of Shârâda Sadan and Mukti

MISS LISSA HASTIE.

Printed in United States of America.